MINECRAFT STEM CHALLENGE

BUILD A CITY

T0027256

THIS IS A CARLTON BOOK

Text, design and illustration
© Carlton Books Limited 2018

Published in 2018 by Carlton Books Limited
An imprint of the Carlton Publishing Group
20 Mortimer Street, London W1T 3JW

A catalogue record for this book is
available from the British Library.

ISBN: 978-1-78312-404-6

Printed in China
3 5 7 9 10 8 6 4

Designed and packaged by:
Dynamo Limited

Built by Jamie Harvey and written by Anne Rooney

The
publishers
would like to thank
the following sources for
their kind permission to reproduce
the pictures in the book.

Key: t = top, b = bottom, c = centre, l = left & r = right

12 Bibiphoto/Shutterstock, 18 © Baycrest, 20
Manekina Serafima/Shutterstock, Boonchuay
Promjiam, 30tl Spencer Platt/Getty Images, bl Punya
Family/Getty Images, br Jonathan Lewis/Getty Images,
32l Pxl.store/Shutterstock, r RastoS/Shutterstock, 33c
Rawpixel.com/Shutterstock, b Jeffrey Greenberg/UIG
via Getty Images, 34 Robert Nickelsberg/Getty Images,
36l Nicholas Rjabow/Shutterstock, r Tymonko Galyna/
Shutterstock, 40 FrameAngel/Shutterstock, 42 Alvinku/
Shutterstock, 46l David McNew/Getty Images, r
Haryigit/Shutterstock, 48 Tovovan/Shutterstock, 60t &
c Martin Janecek/Shutterstock, b Samolevsky/
Shutterstock, 62 Fuhito Kanayama/Getty Images

Every effort has been made to acknowledge correctly
and contact the source and/or copyright holder of each
picture, and Carlton Publishing Group apologizes
for any unintentional errors or omissions,
which will be corrected in future
editions of this book.

MINECRAFT STEM CHALLENGE

BUILD A CITY

CARLTON
BOOKS

CONTENTS

SCIENCE
TECHNOLOGY
ENGINEERING
MATHS

WELCOME TO THE CITY!

Welcome to the world of building in Minecraft. In this book we'll show you how to build an amazing city with a sports stadium, shops, housing, a skyscraper and an underground railway. A real city is huge. We'll start small, but you can keep expanding your city until it's as big as you like.

« TAKE A LOOK »

This is the section of the city we're going to show you how to build. How you develop it after that is entirely up to you.

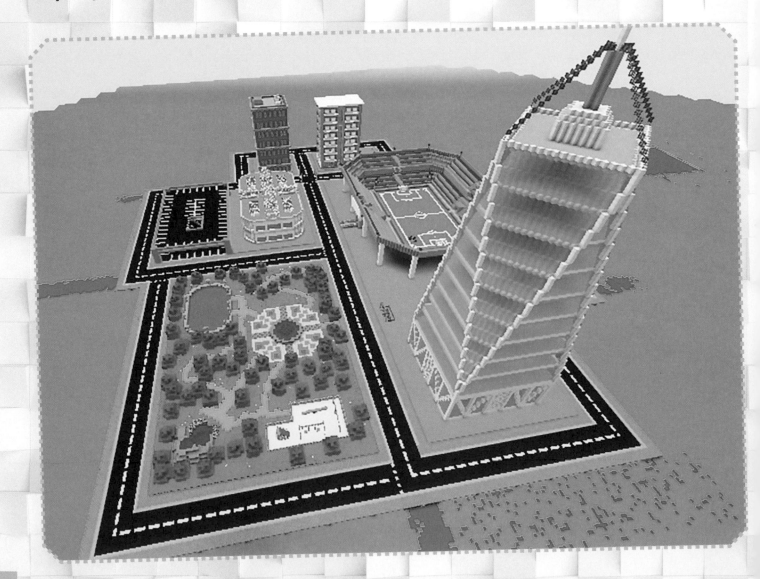

You can make the builds in any order you like. As long as you stick to the plan on the next page, and you make the paved areas and roads that help you put things in the right place, your city will fit together perfectly. There is unlimited space outside to expand it!

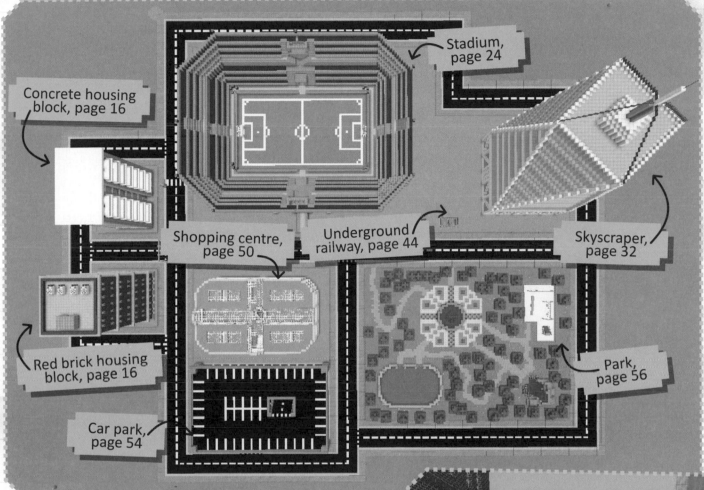

Stadium, page 24

Concrete housing block, page 16

Shopping centre, page 50

Underground railway, page 44

Skyscraper, page 32

Red brick housing block, page 16

Park, page 56

Car park, page 54

« **CITYSCAPE** »

You don't have to make your city look just like this one. Feel free to use different colours and materials. As long as you stick to the basic structure and dimensions so that it all fits and works in the space, you can change the decorations. Your skyscraper could be a surreal construction of lapis lazuli and cobweb. Your park could be a fantasy land full of mushrooms and cacti with a lake of lava. Your road system need not be boring old black and white – It can be any colours you like!

Use WorldEdit to copy and paste buildings to create a whole city

GETTING CREATIVE

If you've only used Minecraft in Survival mode before, you'll be used to having to collect building materials and tools and avoid all kinds of perils to stay alive. Building is a matter of survival and you might have settled for a hut to protect you. If you want to focus on building super structures, you can make life much easier for yourself by working in Creative mode. There will be no hostile mobs out to get you, and you'll have endless supplies of all the materials you want.

« IT'S A FLAT, FLAT WORLD »

It's pretty hard to build a city in the mountains or underwater. Luckily, Minecraft lets you choose a perfectly flat world for building so you don't have to struggle with the wrong type of landscape. Here's how to do it:

Superflat world

STEP 1

At the Select World screen, choose Create New World.

STEP 2

Give your new world a name, then click on the Game Mode button twice until it shows Game Mode: Creative.

STEP 3

Click on the button More World Options.

STEP 4

Click on the World Type button to show the option World Type: Superflat.

STEP 5

Click Done, and then Create New World. Your new world will start with unending views of green grass beneath a blue sky. Time to get building!

STAYING SAFE ONLINE

Minecraft is one of the most popular games in the world, and we want you to have fun while you're playing it. However, it is just as important to stay safe when you're online.

Top tips for staying safe are:

» turn off chat
» find a child-friendly server
» watch out for viruses and malware
» set a game-play time limit
» tell a trusted adult what you're doing.

Courtesy of IAmNewAsWell

CHOOSING MATERIALS

In Creative mode, you don't need to hunt for materials or dig them out of the ground. They are available all the time. Press the E key to bring up the Building Blocks menu. You can pick up to nine materials to have readily to hand and there's no limit to the number of blocks you can use.

GOOD FOUNDATIONS

In real life, buildings aren't plonked straight on top of the ground — they would fall down. They have foundations underground to keep them solid and stable. In a real city, the structures would have poles and pillars going deep into the ground so that they would not fall or blow over and cause accidents. In Minecraft, we don't need to worry about foundations.

GROUND WORK

This plan shows the areas set aside for the different builds. As long as you follow it carefully, your city will come together perfectly. You'll also find a more detailed plan at the start of each build.

ONE STEP AT A TIME

The area on the ground that is occupied by a build is called its footprint.

The underground railway goes underneath the city. The only part that shows on the plan is its entrance.

PERIMETER AND AREA

The perimeter is the total distance around a shape. The city is not a rectangle. If you want to work out its perimeter you have to add up the total length of all its sides:

107 + 42 + 57 + 150 + 32 + 60 + 179 + 113 + 14 + 97 + 61 + 42 = 954 blocks.

The perimeter is a line, so it has one dimension.

The area of a shape is the space it covers. To work out the area of the whole city, we would need to break it down into rectangles, work out the area of each rectangle, and add them all up:

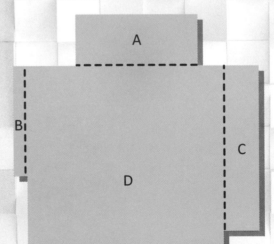

A + B + C + D

Area has two dimensions, so it's usually reported in square units, such as square centimetres (cm²) or square metres (m²).

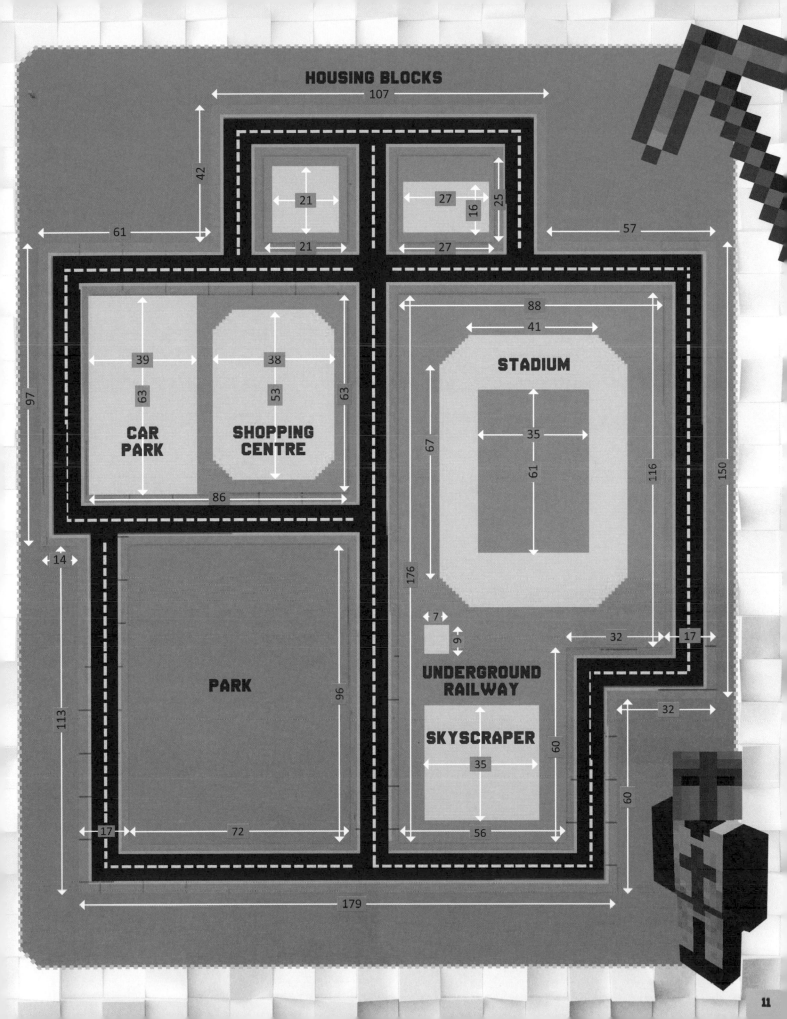

HOUSING BLOCKS

107

42

61

57

21

21

27

27

16

25

97

39

63

38

53

63

88

41

35

61

67

116

150

CAR PARK

SHOPPING CENTRE

STADIUM

86

176

14

7

9

PARK

96

32

17

UNDERGROUND RAILWAY

32

113

60

60

SKYSCRAPER

35

17

72

56

179

PAVING THE WAY

Transport and nature are both really important. In cities, keeping a good balance between roads and green spaces is never easy.

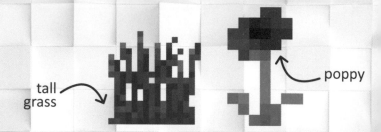

tall grass

poppy

≪
ROAD CONSTRUCTION
≫ ≪
CITIES AND GREEN SPACE
≫

The road in your Minecraft city is concrete laid over clay in a trench. Real roads are also built from layers.

Work starts by digging a trench and making the bottom absolutely flat. Then construction workers tip layers of gravel (small, sharp stones) into the trench and compress it. The top layer is often asphalt, or sometimes concrete. Asphalt is a sticky, oil-based substance called bitumen mixed with sand and bits of rock. It's heated to 150 °C (300 °F) and spread over the gravel layers, then squashed and rolled flat before it cools and hardens. Asphalt is a bit flexible, so the road is unlikely to crack. It softens slightly in the heat, making the sharp smell you sometimes get on hot summer roads.

Modern city planners try to make sure that people and wildlife have some green space, even in cities. Our city has a nice big park. But if you make your city larger, remember to leave extra green areas: sports fields, country parks, public gardens or even a wild bit of woodland.

People who live in cities are healthier if they can get out for some fresh air and enjoy nature. In some countries, cities have a green belt (an area of land that can't be built on) to make sure the city-dwellers can easily get to a natural area.

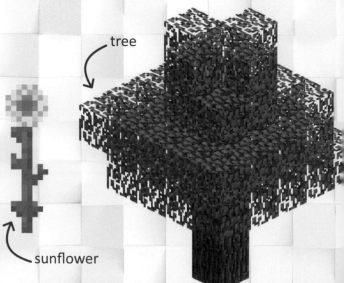

A construction worker laying the asphalt layer of a road.

tree

sunflower

MATERIALS

STEP 1

Begin by marking out the perimeter of the city, using the dimensions in the plan to help you. The dark grey paving around the perimeter is three blocks wide and made from cobblestone slab and stone brick slab arranged in a wavy pattern. The inside edge (or the kerb) is made from stone slab.

STEP 2

Now use the plan to help you lay the roads. Replace grass blocks with black and white concrete so that your roads are lower than your kerbs. Build each road nine blocks wide with dashed white lines down the centre of each. Make each white stripe three blocks long with one black block between each.

STEP 3

Next, add a kerb and dark grey paving along the edges of all of your roads, just the same as you did for the perimeter in Step 1.

STEP 4

Use stone block to cover the rest of the grass inside the perimeter, except for the park.

13

TRANSPORT SYSTEM

A lot of planning goes into roads, from their angles and curves to how the traffic moves along them in the most efficient way. Nobody likes a traffic jam!

 ## BEST BENDS

Real roads don't have corners like right angles. Vehicles could not cope with roads like this. Instead, real roads have rounded corners or slow bends.

To make a curved corner a road engineer has to start curving the road some way back from where the right angle would fall. The further back the curve starts, the gentler it will be. You can think of the curve as being part of a circle. The distance from the centre of a circle to the edge is called the radius. The larger the radius of the circle, the gentler the curve will be, and the safer it will be to drive around.

An engineer's sketch of a curve in the road.

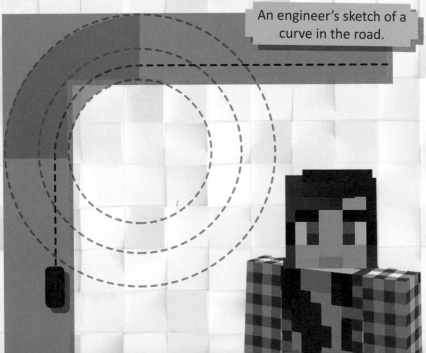

 ## STOP, WAIT, GO!

A **junction** is where roads join one another, giving people a choice of routes. To bring traffic together safely and keep it moving, junctions often use traffic lights or roundabouts to let vehicles take turns.

At **traffic lights**, vehicles stop at a red light and wait for a green light before entering a junction. The lights are set up so that traffic from one direction at a time can go, keeping everyone safe.

At a **roundabout**, vehicles stop or slow down as they come up to a circle of road. They can only drive onto the roundabout if there is no traffic on it already coming towards them. Drivers wait until it's safe, and go round to the exit they want.

STEP 5

Next, add the T-junction markings. Across the roads where drivers have to give way, add a dotted line made from alternate blocks of white and black concrete. The traffic going in a straight line (not having to turn a corner) generally has right of way. Don't forget the entrance to the car park, too.

TOP TIP!

Where roads meet each other, you need to mark the junction so that drivers know whether they are allowed to go straight on or whether they have to give way to traffic coming from another direction.

STEP 6

Create a four-way junction with traffic lights between the housing blocks, the shopping centre and the stadium so the traffic can take turns at moving and not get jammed. Add dotted lines across the end of each of the four roads to form a square where they meet. Knock out a paving slab at each corner and build a column from cobblestone wall seven blocks tall. Join them along the top, using more cobblestone wall. Add two traffic lights on each side, two blocks in from each end, with a gap of three blocks between them. Each traffic light is made of three polished andesite blocks with item frames attached to the front of them, containing red, yellow and lime concrete blocks.

STEP 7

Finally, add a pedestrian crossing so people can cross the road safely. Lay white concrete stripes into the road, one block wide and three blocks long, lined up with one of the centre lines in the road. Then add traffic lights on cobblestone wall columns on each side of the road.

HIGH-RISE HOUSING

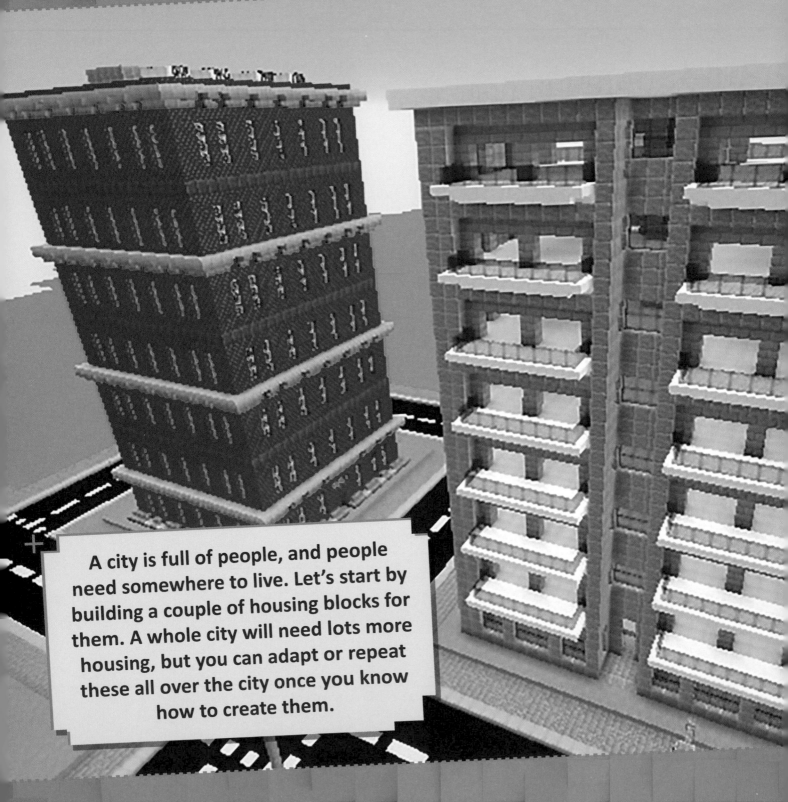

A city is full of people, and people need somewhere to live. Let's start by building a couple of housing blocks for them. A whole city will need lots more housing, but you can adapt or repeat these all over the city once you know how to create them.

Here's the layout for the apartment blocks. Look carefully at the plan and refer back to it as you are building. It has all the dimensions you will need to use. The plan is shown to scale. Your build will have exactly the same proportions as the picture in the plan.

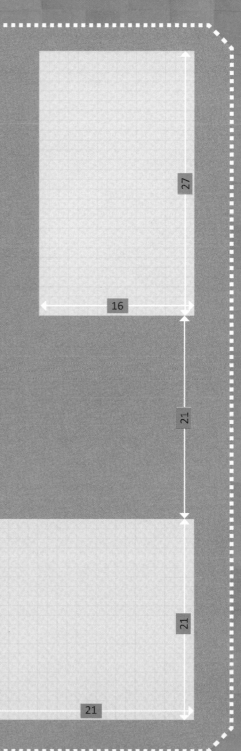

LIVING ROOM

In cities, many people live in blocks of flats or apartments as more people can fit into the same area of ground than if they live in houses. The materials that are used need to keep people safe as well as give them a good quality of life.

bricks

stone block

white concrete

 ## TALL ORDER

Most buildings are made of bricks, stone or concrete as these are hard materials that stand up to extreme weather and last a long time. You don't want buildings to fall down in a high wind or to dissolve in the rain! It's important to choose materials with the properties important for the purpose; bricks, stone and granite are ideal for your first housing block.

SPACED OUT

A house with an area of 10x20 blocks can house a family of four. A housing block with an area of 20x20 blocks can house two families of four on each floor. So, a housing block with six floors can house 48 people. To work out how many families can live in a building, calculate the volume of the building

height x width x length

and divide this by the space needed to house each family.

Tall buildings, like this skyscraper, save a lot of space on the ground and can accommodate thousands of people.

STEP 1

Refer to the plan for the whole city so you start in the right place. In the centre of the 29x29 paved area where your red brick block of flats is going to go, build a 21x21 square outline for the outside walls. Leave an opening for the door in the middle of the front wall, then build the walls five blocks high leaving space for the windows in each side.

STEP 2

Add stone brick stair in front of the wall, but use stone slabs in front of each window. Don't block the door!

STEP 3

Before you build the next storey, add a layer of polished granite to the top of the brick. Then build up the window pillars to match the ground floor. Above the front door, add another window instead of a door.

STEP 4

Place upside-down stone brick stair on the outside of the granite, but leave a space above the windows. Then add a layer of stone slabs on top of the stair all around the building to make a ledge.

STEP 5

Add another row of polished granite slabs all around the top of the wall, and continue the brickwork to make a third storey. You can repeat this step as many times as you like to make your apartment block as tall as you want it to be.

WHAT A SIGHT!

If we live in a place that looks nice, we feel happy. You could say, the things we surround ourselves with are pretty important! Even in nature, symmetry is a sign of beauty.

« CLEAR VIEW »

Glass is translucent, which means it lets light through. Just what you need for windows! Materials that don't let light through are opaque — like the walls of this building.

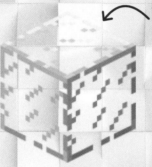

glass block

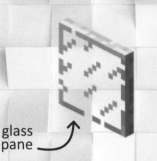

glass pane

« SYMMETRY »

A symmetrical shape is one that has matching halves. It can be folded in half exactly so that one half covers the other. The letter 'E' is symmetrical from top to bottom; fold it in half horizontally and the shape of both halves is the same. The letter 'A' is symmetrical from left to right; fold it vertically and both sides match.

Butterflies are a perfect example of vertical symmetry in nature.

A square has left-right and up-down symmetry, and it also has diagonal symmetry. A rectangle has left-right and up-down symmetry, but does not have diagonal symmetry. Because it's square, the plan for the red brick block of flats has left-right, up-down and diagonal symmetry. The plan for the grey block of flats has left-right and up-down symmetry.

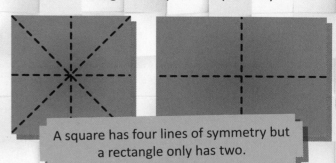

A square has four lines of symmetry but a rectangle only has two.

« INTERIORS »

In a real apartment block, there would be internal walls and doors, stairs between the floors and a lift shaft. You could add these inside your apartment block if you like. Builders make important structural walls while they are building the outside, but add doors, stairs and internal walls afterwards. You could even decorate the rooms with paintings, bookshelves and furniture when you have finished.

painting

bookshelf

20

STEP 6

Every second floor, add the decorative stone border again. Inside, add a floor of oak wood plank at the level of each row of granite blocks. Then add glass pane to all the windows.

STEP 7

Finally, add a roof made from stone slab. On top of this add a 3x7 elevator box and four 2x3 air-conditioning units. The elevator is made of polished andesite with an iron door. The air-con units are made of iron blocks with iron bars in front, with a circle of curved rail and a piece of powered rail on top.

STEP 8

Build the second housing block just across the street from the first one. Dig a 27x16 rectangle two blocks deep in the 31x25 paved area. Leave a rim two blocks wide at the front and sides and seven blocks wide at the back. Line the floor with stone brick.

STEP 9

Start building the ground floor. There are a lot of windows in these apartments that we need to leave space for. Make the front and back walls and the top rows along the side walls from polished andesite. Use quartz blocks for the side walls and the top rows above the windows at the front and back. Lay oak wood plank flooring throughout.

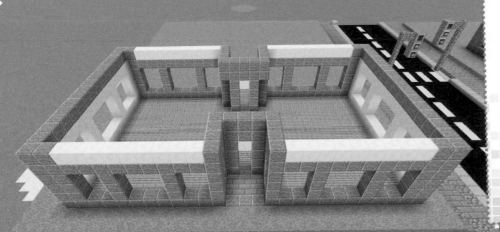

ROTATE AND TRANSLATE

Understanding how to copy and repeat shapes is vital in real-life construction as well as when you're building in Minecraft.

《 BACK TO FRONT 》

The front of the concrete housing block is a mirror image of the back. If you put a mirror across the middle of the block, from left to right, the reflection in the mirror looks exactly the same as the back of the block.

When an object is reflected, its left-hand side appears on the right, and its right-hand side appears on the left (or its top appears at the bottom and its bottom at the top). The reflection is the same distance from the mirror line as the the object.

Symmetrical shape	Reflection

Asymmetrical shape	Reflection

《 DO YOU COPY? 》

Reflection is one type of transformation. Other types are translation and rotation.

A translated shape is exactly the same as the original, but moved to a different place. It is not rotated, resized or reflected.

These housing blocks, facing the same direction but in different places, are an example of translation.

A rotated object is turned around. It is not changed or moved in any other way.

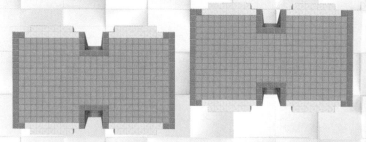

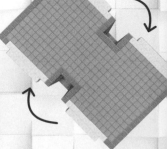

These housing blocks, facing in different directions, are an example of rotation.

STEP 10

Now we'll add the next floor. Begin by creating a floor of stone slabs, with a single row of quartz front and back. Then add an overhanging row of quartz, two blocks shorter, above the windows front and back. These will form the balconies in the finished block.

STEP 11

Next, build up the walls for this storey using polished andesite and stone brick. They are one block in from the walls below.

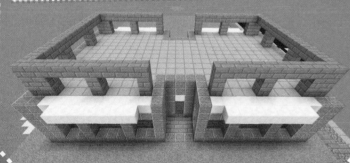

STEP 12

The people who live in these apartments will enjoy sitting on their balconies watching the city. Put a row of quartz slabs around the quartz blocks and add glass panes to the slabs. These will stop people falling off the balconies, but they will still be able to see through them.

STEP 13

Add a layer of polished andesite blocks all around the outside walls (but not the balcony columns) to make the walls flush with those on the ground floor. Then create balconies using black stained glass pane.

STEP 14

Repeat Steps 10-13 to add as many more floors as you want. When you've finished, use quartz blocks to make the roof.

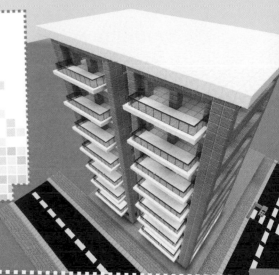

STADIUM

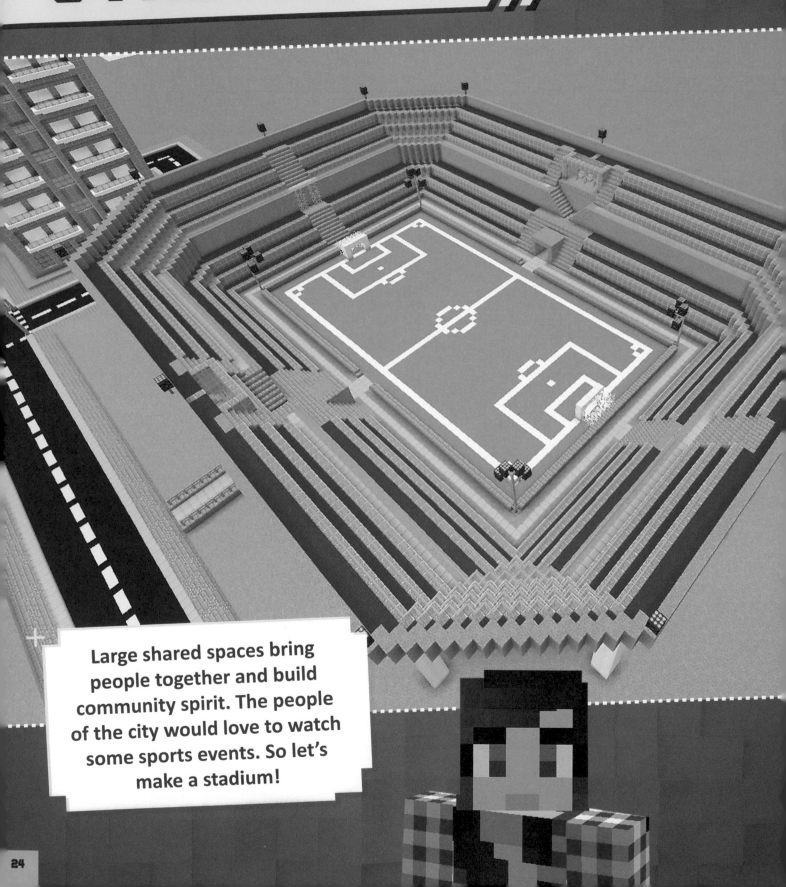

Large shared spaces bring people together and build community spirit. The people of the city would love to watch some sports events. So let's make a stadium!

This is a football pitch. If you'd like to watch a different game, use WORKING WITH SCALE on page 26 to help you work out the new dimensions you will need.

TOP TIP!

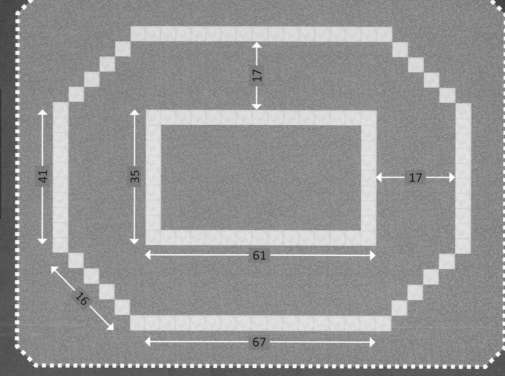

MATERIALS

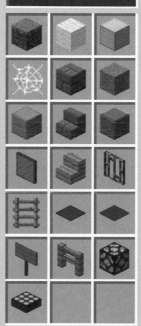

PITCH PERFECT

Here's the plan for the stadium. It has a football pitch in the middle, and stands for spectators all around the sides. Refer back to the plan as you build, making sure you get all the dimensions right for the tunnels, stands and commentators' boxes. You can make the stadium slightly wider or narrower if you want to have a different type of pitch but try to keep the length about the same.

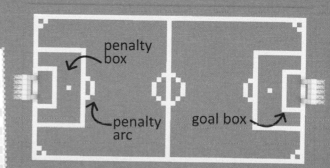

STEP 1

Using the city plan as a guide, build a 35x61 rectangle of grass block on top of your stone paving. Mark out a 31x57 rectangle on top of it with white wool. Divide it down the middle and add a circle with a diameter of seven blocks in the centre. Make 5x9 goal boxes, 11x17 penalty boxes and 3x5 penalty arcs. Build two goals, each five blocks wide and three blocks tall, from iron block with cobweb nets.

THE SHAPE OF THINGS TO COME

Understanding shapes and sizes is essential when you're building.

《 CIRCLES AND LINES 》

Circumference

Radius

Diameter

The perimeter of a circle is called its circumference. The line drawn through the centre of a circle to the circumference is its diameter. The diameter is the same length wherever you draw it. The diameter always cuts the circle in half. A line from the edge of a circle to the middle is called the radius, and is half the diameter.

《 WORKING WITH SCALE 》

If you want to use your stadium for a different game, you'll need to change the markings and possibly the size. Try to keep the length about the same, so that it still fits inside its footprint in your plan of the city.

Your football pitch takes up an area of 35x61.

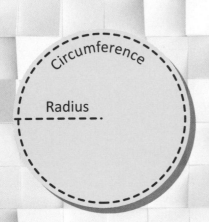

A doubles tennis court is 11 m (36 f) x 24 m (78 f).

If you multiply 11 by 3, you get 33 and if you multiply 24 by 3 you get 72.

A good scale to use could be 1 m: 3 blocks.

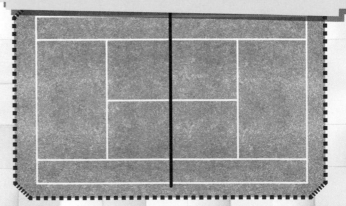

A hockey field is 55 m (60 yards) x 92 m (100 yards).

If you halve 60, you get 30 and if you halve 100, you get 50.

A good scale to use could be 1 yard: 0.5 blocks.

STEP 2

Around the perimeter of the 35x61x1 grass rectangle, add a row of stone brick two blocks high and a row of stone, a row of double stone slab and another row of stone slab all one block high.

STEP 3

Opposite the centre line halfway down the pitch, remove seven blocks from the wall and add stone brick stair either side of the gap. Replace 3x4 of the path with double stone slab. Replace 3x7 grass blocks with stone brick to create a path. Then build a 5x4 tunnel over the path from stone brick and stone.

STEP 4

Now build the stands. On each side of the tunnel, add diagonal rows of stone brick stair. Make these four blocks long and five blocks high. Either side of the stair, make the stands from polished andesite. Each layer is two blocks deep and two blocks high. Add light grey stained glass pane along the front of each stand as a safety barrier.

glass safety barrier

STEP 5

Extend the top of the stairs using stone brick to make a platform that is five blocks deep. Build two sets of steps up from the middle of the platform. Make them three blocks wide and four blocks high. At the top of each set of stairs, build a walkway from stone and double stone slab. Extend it to the end of the stands.

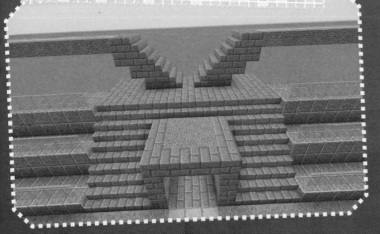

STEP 6

Fill in the wall between the new path and the stand below. Then add grey stained glass along the front edge of the path. Then build another two sets of stairs, three blocks wide and five blocks high, with a row of stone brick between them.

The seats in the stadium are tiered; they are higher up further from the sports field and lower down nearer the field. This means people at the back still have a good view. They need a clear line of sight to see the game, without the heads of people in front blocking their view.

We could have built a rectangular stadium but this wouldn't have given customers in the corners a very good view because they would have had to turn at an angle to see the pitch. We don't fit quite as many spectators in with the arrangement we've chosen, but at least they won't grumble!

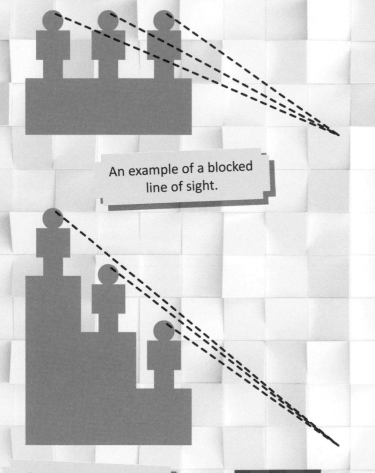

An example of a blocked line of sight.

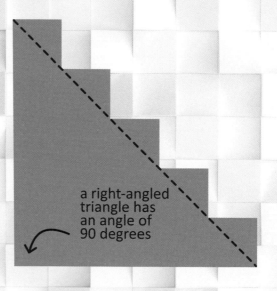

a right-angled triangle has an angle of 90 degrees

We removed the shape of a right-angled triangle from the four corners of the stadium.

An example of a clear line of sight.

You can work out the length of the long side (called the hypotenuse) if you know the lengths of the other two sides.

$$(a \times a) + (b \times b) = (c \times c)$$

This can be written as:

$$a^2 + b^2 = c^2$$

In our triangles, a and b are the same length.

STEP 7

The commentator's box will fit in the gap between the staircases. Make it 9x4x4, using stone with polished andesite at the front. Use oak wood stair for the commentators' chairs and give them microphones made of iron bars. Cover the front with grey stained glass pane; it cuts glare and gives the commentators a good view of the pitch.

STEP 8

Make stands for this second tier, the same as on the lower level, on either side of the stairs.

STEP 9

On the opposite side of the stadium, repeat Steps 3-8 so the stands looks exactly the same.

STEP 10

Now make the stands at the ends of the pitch, behind the goals. Add a staircase in the middle, five blocks wide and five blocks high, with stands of the same design on either side.

STEP 11

At the back of the last stand, build a wall four blocks high and three blocks deep using stone and double stone slab. Add ladders above the steps and finish with a safety barrier made from grey stained glass pane.

glass safety barrier

STEP 12

Then starting from the landing behind the ladders, add another staircase, five blocks wide and five blocks high. Build stands either side of this, as before.

SAFE AND SOUND

The support structure is one of the most important features of a real building, something you'll never have to worry about in Minecraft. Lighting, on the other hand, is vital in both places.

≪ SUPPORTING A BUILDING ≫

≪ AUTOMATIC LIGHTING ≫

A real stadium couldn't be built in this sequence. The stands would not be stable unless supports were added at the start. A stadium like this would have much more support, with supporting walls beneath the tiers of the stands.

Lights that turn on automatically when it starts to get dark respond to the amount of light falling on a sensor. Often, people have garden or patio lights that come on in the evening. Motion sensors are also often used with lights. These respond to movement nearby to turn on a security light. In both cases, a sensor picks up a stimulus (falling light levels, or movement) and triggers a switch in an electric circuit.

Some columns go deep into the ground while others support the building above ground level.

When the light level falls, the sensor outside this house triggers a switch to turn on the lights.

Horizontal support structures give columns extra strength.

daylight sensor

STEP 13

Your stadium now has four sides, but there are big gaps in the corners! Fill these in by adding one extra block to the back row of each stand and then laying blocks, corner-to-corner, across the gap to join up the stands at each level.

STEP 14

Fill in the gaps to extend the stands around the corner. Don't forget to add the safety barrier! The stands and the safety barrier will have a zig-zag pattern. Add a wall two blocks high behind the highest stand – we don't want anyone to fall off.

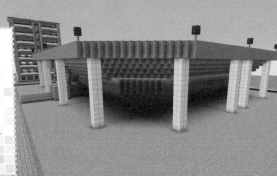

STEP 15

We're going to keep supporters of the competing teams separate. To make sure everyone knows where to go, colour-code the two halves of the stadium by laying carpet on the stands.

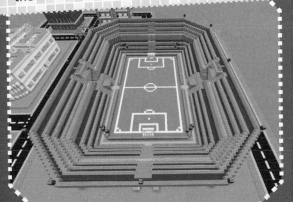

STEP 16

This stadium is hanging in mid-air at the moment, and that's not very safe. Add two 2x2x14 iron block supports at each corner and in the middle of each side.

STEP 17

Build hollow 5x4x3 ticket booths at the ends of the entrance tunnels from Step 3. Use polished andesite, iron bar and signs. Add turnstiles made from iron bar and fence. Add a path to the pavement using oak fence, stone slab and stone brick.

STEP 18

Finally, in each corner of the pitch and in the top corners of the stands, add lighting made from redstone lamps, daylight sensors and fence. Right-click the daylight sensor to set your lights to turn on at night.

SKYSCRAPER

Modern cities are famous for their skyscrapers. They even compete with each other for the biggest, most dramatic and most bizarre designs. Most new skyscrapers are spectacular constructions of glass and steel – and that's what you're going to add to your city now.

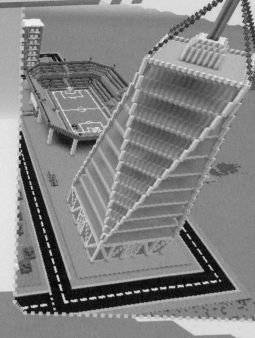

The Shard, London

≪ PERFECT ≫ PLACE

The skyscraper is across the road from the park. This means workers can go for a walk outside in their lunch break. It's right next to the entrance to the underground railway so that people can easily get to and from work.

The Burj Khalifa, Dubai

MATERIALS

(materials crafting grid)

35

35

A skyscraper can accommodate many workers within a small area because it stretches up towards the sky.

The viewing platform at the top of a skyscraper is a great way to see the layout of a city.

≪ WHAT'S INSIDE? ≫

Most skyscrapers contain offices where people work. Some are occupied by just one large organisation, such as a bank or a government department. Others are divided up so several different organisations share the building.

Although lots of space is used for offices, there is usually room for coffee shops, restaurants and perhaps even a gym for the people who work there. Some skyscrapers have shops at the bottom. A few have restaurants or viewing platforms at the very top, giving spectacular views over the city.

STRONG STRUCTURES

You don't need foundations or strong shapes for your Minecraft builds but in the real world they are essential.

≪ FIRM FOUNDATIONS ≫

Constant vibrations from heavy traffic and underground railways plus high winds and even earthquakes threaten the stability of skyscrapers, so they need solid foundations.

The foundations for a house might consist of a pit filled with rubble but for a skyscraper the builders might dig all the way down to rock to provide a solid base. They might drive long, thick metal columns, called piles, deep into the ground to support the structure.

Once the piles have been driven deep into the ground, builders can lay the building's foundations.

≪ THE MIGHTY TRIANGLE ≫

Some shapes are stronger or more stable than others. If you push on one side of a rectangle, it's quite easy to bend it out of shape. The angles between its sides can change, turning it into a parallelogram. The structure can fail even though the sides don't come apart.

Force

Triangles aren't easily distorted like this. Pushing on one side of a triangle doesn't alter the angles.

Force

Triangles are strong shapes that are difficult to distort. When creating a building in the real world, architects and engineers have to think about the kinds of pressures and stresses that could damage the building. Diagonal struts are often used to turn large rectangles into triangles.

STEP 1

Using the city plan as a guide, mark out the 35x35 square base of the skyscraper, using iron block set into the ground. Start building in the large paved space next to the stadium.

TOP TIP!

Add a pattern to your floor as well as your walls. Use several of the 16 different coloured hardened clays Minecraft has to offer to create a stunning modern mosaic.

STEP 2

Using iron blocks, build the frame for your first section. Make it 14 blocks high with columns in each corner. Build another four columns along each side, with a gap of five blocks between the two central columns and six between the rest. Add four diagonal struts between the columns on each wall to make V-shapes. Create a geometric pattern between the two central columns on each wall.

STEP 3

Fill in all the gaps with light blue stained glass block. Leave a central doorway two blocks tall in the middle of each side.

doorway

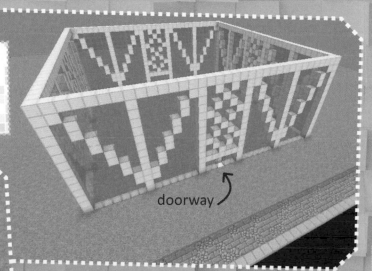

doorway

35

SUPPORT STRUCTURES

In Minecraft builds, no structural support is needed. A single layer of blocks can form the ceiling and the floor above it. Not so in real life...

⟪ ABOVE AND BELOW ⟫

In a real building, the ceiling and floor are separate, with a space between. Joists are laid across the building between the walls. The ceiling is fastened to the lower surface of the joists, and the floor to the upper surface. Insulation placed in this gap helps to stop heat moving up through the building and also provides soundproofing between floors.

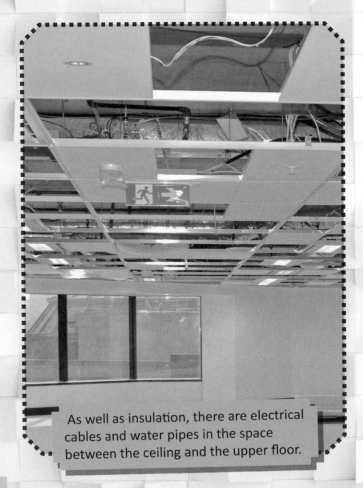

As well as insulation, there are electrical cables and water pipes in the space between the ceiling and the upper floor.

⟪ LONG AND STRONG ⟫

Columns have been used to hold up parts of buildings for thousands of years. They can support a roof without the need for solid walls all the way round a building. Ancient Greek and Roman temples and other buildings had columns of special designs called Doric, Ionian and Corinthian.

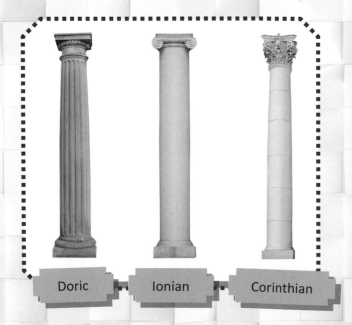

Doric | Ionian | Corinthian

A Doric column is wider at the bottom than at the top, and is the strongest type. It has no separate base. The other two types are the same width all the way up and stand on a base. Columns are still used in modern buildings, often when there are no internal walls. You can often see them in large, open buildings like car parks and airports.

STEP 4

Fill in the space between the iron blocks at the top with double stone slab to make a ceiling and a floor.

STEP 5

Inside the building, add a white concrete pillar in the middle, going from the floor to the ceiling. Then build four light grey concrete pillars around it, one at each corner.

STEP 6

Three blocks out from the central pillar, make a reception desk from a 9x9 square made from cobblestone wall topped with stone slab that goes all around the pillar.

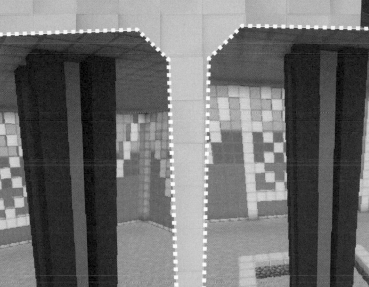

STEP 7

Back outside, create the iron block frame for the next floor. Add a 4x1 column to each corner of the building. Then place two more 4x1 columns diagonally on top of each column. Placing the blocks diagonally like this is the first step towards creating triangle-shaped walls. Link the corner columns with rows of blocks.

SHAPES AND STRUCTURES

Buildings contain many different shapes. These shapes work together to give each building its own look.

≪ SKY-SHAPE-ER ≫

▶ SQUARE

The base of the skyscraper is a square.

- four equal sides
- four right (90 degree) angles

▶ RECTANGLE

If the skyscraper had vertical sides, they would be rectangular.

- sides of two different lengths
- four right (90 degree) angles

But as you build this skyscraper higher, instead of vertical sides you build diagonal sides.

▶ ISOSCELES TRIANGLE

Eventually the sides meet in a point at the top to form isosceles triangles, with two equal angles and two equal sides.

- three sides
- angles that add up to 180 degrees

≪ POLYGONS ≫

A multi-sided shape is called a polygon. Polygons can be regular or irregular. A square and an equilateral triangle are both regular polygons. A rectangle and an isosceles triangle are both examples of irregular polygons. An irregular polygon has some sides of unequal length, even if a few are equal.

As the diagonal sides of your skyscraper grow, the skyscraper's floor shape changes from a square to an irregular octagon. Halfway up, it will be a regular octagon, with eight equal sides. Then it will be an irregular octagon through the following floors until it's square again.

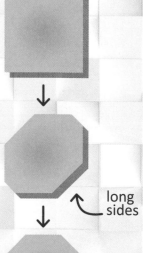
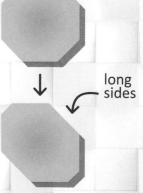

long sides

long sides

This sequence shows the changing floor shape of your skyscraper.

STEP 8

Fill in the walls with light blue stained glass and add a ceiling made from double stone slab.

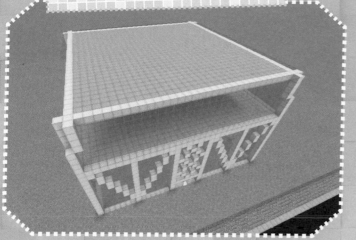

STEP 9

Repeat Step 5 to create the pillar in the centre of the floor.

STEP 10

Repeat Steps 7-9 to build the next floor. At the corners, place columns diagonally on top of the previous ones to make the triangle-shaped walls grow with each new floor.

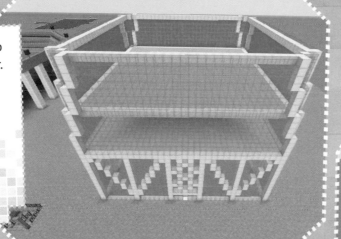

STEP 11

Keep on adding more floors by repeating Steps 7-9. The upside down (inverted) triangles will get wider as the width of the adjacent sides reduces.

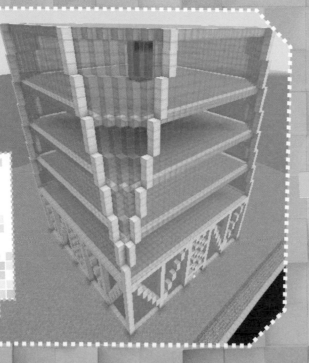

STEP 12

As you keep going, you will notice that the ceilings you are filling in are no longer square. You have cut the corners off the skyscraper making the inverted triangles, so the floors are becoming octagonal.

HIGH AND MIGHTY

The triangular sides of your skyscraper make it very strong and its towering walls of glass will always stay clean. But what do we do in the real world to make sure skyscrapers stay dirt-free?

« SQUEAKY CLEAN »

Most skyscrapers have a lot of glass, and that means they take a lot of cleaning! Windows get dirty from rain mixed with dust in the air, from bird droppings and from pollution. It would soon be hard to see through the windows if they weren't cleaned.

Many are still cleaned by brave, expert window cleaners working from platforms or wires hundreds of metres above the ground. Others are cleaned by special machines. But some skyscrapers have self-cleaning glass. This has a special coating that reacts with sunlight to break down and loosen dirt. Then, when it rains, the rain spreads over the whole window like a sheet of water and washes away the loose dirt. No one needs to do anything!

Workers clean the outside of a skyscraper.

« THE BIG THREE »

» ISOSCELES

The triangles on the sides of your skyscraper are isosceles triangles. Isosceles triangles have two sides of the same length and one side of a different length. Two of their angles are the same, and one is different. They can be tall and thin, or short and squat.

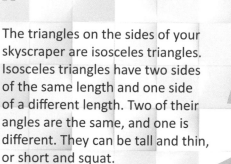

» EQUILATERAL

A triangle with all three sides the same length also has three angles the same. It's called an equilateral triangle.

» RIGHT-ANGLED TRIANGLE

A triangle that has a right angle (90 degrees) is a right-angled triangle. If both the other angles are 45 degrees, it's also an isosceles triangle.

STEP 13

Eventually, the sides will narrow into points and the corners will widen into long edges.

STEP 14

Keep repeating Steps 7-9 until each side reaches a point, the corners become the sides and the ceiling is square again!

TOP TIP!

You'll notice all the blocks are now lying diagonally. This is because the square roof has turned through 45 degrees and it doesn't line up with the square base.

top floor overlapping ground floor

STEP 15

People will need to go onto the roof, so we'd better make it safe. Build a wall one block tall all around the top edge, over the top of the blue glass blocks.

STEP 16

In the centre of the roof, build a 7x7x4 cuboid using iron block. This is the base for the radio antennae.

HIDDEN POWERS

Skyscrapers are great places to send clear radio signals from. They are also more flexible than you might think – they can sway gently from side to side in the wind.

« WAVES IN SPACE »

« BENDY BUILDINGS »

Radio waves are waves of electromagnetic energy. Other types of electromagnetic waves include light, X-rays and microwaves (the same as in a microwave oven). Radio waves can travel through air or space, but they can be stopped by some materials, such as the steel structure of a building.

Radio antennae are often put on top of skyscrapers because they are taller than the other buildings around them. Up high there is very little to interfere with the radio waves.

The tops of some skyscrapers can move from side to side by up to a metre in really strong winds. This isn't dangerous, in fact it makes the building safer because some movement in one part of the building stops the whole building feeling the full force of the wind. Many skyscrapers are now built with tuned mass dampers at the top. Tuned mass dampers stay still, like an anchor, while the rest of the building moves in response to wind or earth tremors. Their heavy suspended weight absorbs and balances the movement of the earth or the wind to help keep the building steady.

The tuned mass damper inside the Taipei 101 skyscraper.

radio waves

STEP 17

One block in from the top edge of the base, add a 6x6 layer of blocks. On top of that add another layer, this time 5x5, to complete the roof.

STEP 18

In the middle of the roof, use five grey concrete blocks to make a cross-shape. Build this 10 blocks high to create the first section of your radio antenna.

STEP 19

Add a 10x1 column made from iron block to create the second section of the antennae.

STEP 20

On top of the thinner column, add the antenna itself. This is made of iron bar and is five blocks tall. The antenna could still blow around and bend or break in high winds. Add strong cables to hold it in position through the fiercest storms. Use iron bar to connect the middle of the antenna support to the corners of the building to keep it secure and stable.

UNDERGROUND RAILWAY

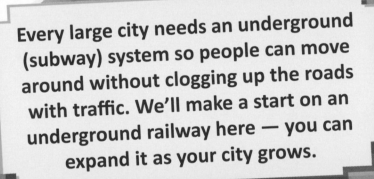

Every large city needs an underground (subway) system so people can move around without clogging up the roads with traffic. We'll make a start on an underground railway here — you can expand it as your city grows.

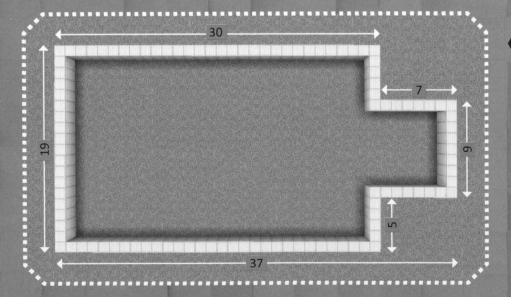

30

7

19

9

5

37

DOWN UNDER

Unlike the other builds, most of this is underground. All kinds of buildings go above underground railways. This is the plan for the railway station you will build. Remember that only the entrance will be visible above ground.

≪ UNDER THE CITY ≫

People began building underground railway systems in the 1800s. The trains in those days were all coal-driven steam trains, so the tunnels were dirty, smoky and smelly. Today, underground trains run on electric lines. They're cleaner and quieter and safer. City planners work out where people want to go and engineers work out the best routes. Above ground, people can change direction and choose to go by different roads. Below ground, they can only stay on the train and go where the train goes, so it needs to go to the right places!

Start by building above the ground, making the entrance to the first station. We'll put it next to the sports stadium, as lots of people will want to go there.

sign

MATERIALS

TOP TIP!

Use signs to provide directions and also to give each of your stations a name.

STEP 1

First dig a hole nine blocks wide, seven blocks long and five blocks deep. Line three sides of the top of the hole with polished andesite. Decorate the last side with an archway made from cobblestone wall and build steps down from it using five stone brick stair blocks placed corner to corner. Add a line of polished andesite blocks down the centre with iron bars on top for railings. Then line the sides of the stairs with stone block.

STEP 2

Now, two blocks down from the bottom of your steps, hollow out a hole nineteen blocks wide (six blocks out from either side of your steps), 30 blocks long and six blocks high (stop one block below the surface). Line your hole with stone and add a seven block wide platform all the way down the middle.

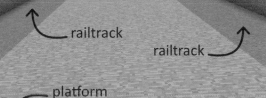

railtrack

railtrack

platform

ROCK AND ROLL

There are different ways of building an underground rail network but the completed rail systems run on the same thing: electricity.

DIGGING TUNNELS

There are two main ways to build tunnels in the real world.

One way is to open up the ground and build the tunnel in a trench, then cover it over again afterwards. This is the cheapest and easiest way. But that's not possible in a city that has already been built, where all the ground is occupied.

The other way is to use a massive boring machine (because it bores a hole, not because it's dull). This machine grinds away the spoil (dirt and rock) in front of it and moves slowly forward into the space it has excavated. The spoil is carried from the front of the machine to the back to be taken away.

Spoil coming out of the back end of a boring machine as it drills a hole underground.

All tunnels need strong supports in the walls and roof to prevent them collapsing inwards. The weight of soil, rock and buildings above a tunnel puts a lot of pressure on the roof, so it needs to be really strong.

ELECTRIC RAILS

Real underground trains run on electric rails. Electricity can only flow through a completed circuit.

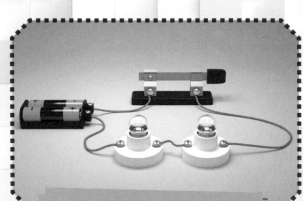

A circuit needs a source of power (such as a battery) and components (such as copper wire) to conduct electricity.

An underground rail network is a much larger electrical circuit. Instead of wire, metal tracks carry electricity. To complete the circuit, the train makes contact with a 'third rail' which lies between or alongside the two main rails. The train acts like a switch, completing or breaking the circuit to make power flow or stop. When the circuit is complete, the electricity drives the train's motors and that turns the wheels – and the train moves.

STEP 3

Line the side of the tunnel with quartz block. Add a row of stone brick stair at the bottom. Two blocks up, add another row, this time upside down. At the top, add a row of stone brick slabs, two blocks wide.

stone brick slab

stone brick stair (upside down)

stone brick stair

STEP 4

The trains will run on powered rails. Replace the stone floor next to the stone brick stair with redstone blocks and lay powered rail on top. The redstone will provide power to the rails to move the minecarts.

STEP 5

Lay a row of stone brick stair along the other side of the track. Then replace the row of stone at the edge of the platform with yellow concrete. This line marks the edge of the platform so that passengers can see it clearly and won't fall onto the rails.

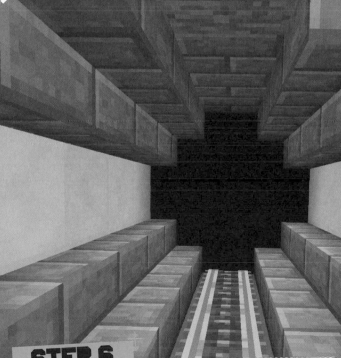

STEP 6

At the end of the platform, continue the tunnel walls by extending the three rows of stone brick stair and adding another row two blocks above platform level to create a rounded tunnel for your track to run along. Remove the blocks inside your tunnel walls to create your tunnel. Make it as long as you want to.

REFLECT AND CONNECT

Light is scarce underground but there are clever ways to increase light levels, and planning your underground system carefully could help with this.

« LIGHT, DARK AND COLOURS »

Have you noticed that a room painted white seems much lighter than a room painted a dark colour, even if they are both the same size and have the same windows or lighting? That's because pale colours, and particularly white, reflect a lot of light. The light bounces off the pale walls and makes the room lighter. If the walls are dark, they absorb light.

When you look at a coloured object, the colour you see is the light reflected from the surface. So a red rug absorbs light of lots of colours, but reflects red light. White light is a mix of all colours, as you can tell if you split it into a spectrum. (A rainbow works in the same way: the water drops split the light into its different colours.) By giving your station a white roof, you will help to keep it light and it will reflect the light coming from the glowstone lamps.

« EXTEND YOUR RAILS »

You can make more stations in exactly the same way at other locations in your city. If you want to join up the stations, you will need to plan the route carefully before you begin. Use squared paper to draw a scale plan of the city, then draw in the route you want your railway line to take and where you will put the stations.

It's easiest to make a single straight line that joins all your stations, running from one end of the city to the other. You will need to count carefully as you dig the tunnels to make sure everything joins up properly.

Make sure you build the entrances facing the right way, so that the platform is between the two tracks and not across them!

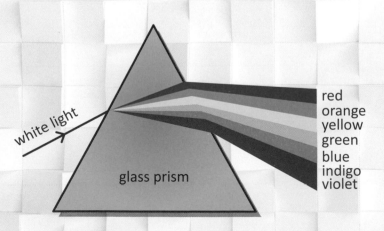

white light

glass prism

red
orange
yellow
green
blue
indigo
violet

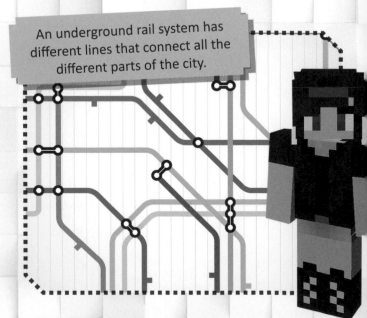

An underground rail system has different lines that connect all the different parts of the city.

STEP 7

Repeat Steps 3-6 on the other side of the platform (and at the other ends of the platforms) so that rails and tunnels on both sides continue in both directions. Note: from this angle you can't see the redstone tracks but don't worry, they are there!

STEP 8

You need to make sure that the roof is not going to fall in on the unfortunate passengers! Every six blocks on both sides of the platform, use iron block to build columns to support the roof.

STEP 8

As it is, this won't be a very nice station to wait in. It will be dark underground, and there's nowhere to sit. Let's make it nicer. Change the ceiling to quartz, which is lighter and will reflect more light down to the platform. Then mid-way between each pair of roof supports, hang a glowstone block from the ceiling to provide lighting. Use quartz slab to build benches three blocks long between the supports, remembering to leave a gap each end so that people can walk through to get on the trains.

SHOPPING CENTRE

People in your city will want somewhere to buy the things that they need so let's give them a shopping centre. This one will go next to your red brick housing block, across the road from your stadium. It's light and airy – the perfect place to shop.

≪ SHOP FLOORS ≫

This is the plan for the shopping centre. There are two floors with the same layout, except that the second floor doesn't have doors to the outside world.

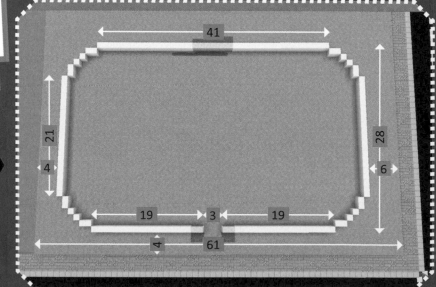

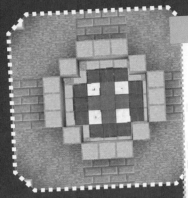

STEP 1

With the plan as your guide, start laying the outside walls of the shopping centre using quartz block. Leave a gap at the front for the entrance. Then mark out the internal walls and add paths using double stone slab.

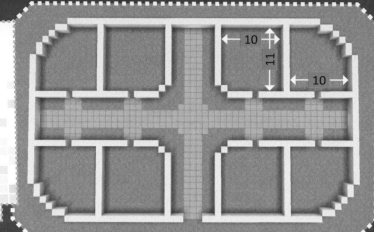

10
11
10

MATERIALS

STEP 2

Add a fountain in the middle of the shopping centre. Use quartz stair for the base, with pillar quartz in the centre. Add glass pane around the top edge of the quartz stair; this will make the water flow the way you want it to later on. Add stone slabs around the bottom of the fountain to contain the falling water and stop it from going everywhere! Add water by tapping the top of the fountain with a water bucket.

STEP 3

Now build a framework for all of the walls using more quartz. Make it five blocks high, leaving big spaces for the windows. Shops have large display windows to attract customers. Remember to leave doorways in the internal walls so that people can get into the shops. The doorways to each shop line up with the paths. Add a row of pillar quartz above the main entrance.

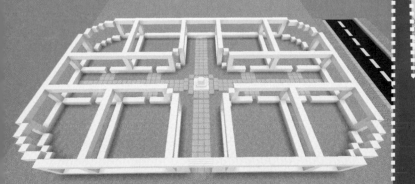

STEP 4

Now add pillar quartz to either side of each shop doorway. Then add the windows. Fill in all the large windows with glass pane. Where there are gaps at the corners of walls, use glass blocks because you can't place glass pane across a diagonal.

SHAPE AND MATTER

Rounded shapes and water features are both possible in the blocky world of Minecraft – they just take planning and preparation.

≪ MAKING CURVES ≫

The shops have curved corners, but these are not easy to make with only straight-sided bricks. You can think of a curved line as being made up of lots of very tiny short straight lines. When the lines are short enough, the line looks curved, but if you zoom in or make the lines longer, it gets blocky.

In Minecraft, all curves are blocky. If you want to plan a build with curved lines, the best way to work out the curves is to use graph paper.

≪ SOLID, LIQUID, GAS ≫

There are three states in which matter exists in the world around us. It can be a solid, a liquid or a gas. All the blocks you have used so far are solids. Solids hold their own shape. Liquids don't hold their own shape, so have to be held in a container. The fountain has a low wall around it as otherwise the water would flow all over the floor, as it would in real life. Liquids flow downhill. A gas does not hold its own shape but will fill any space it is in. While liquids flow downwards, gases usually spread out in all directions.

Colouring in the blocks that your curved shape goes through provides a plan for your Minecraft build.

← water block

← grass block

STEP 5

Customers will need to be able to go up to the next floor. Opposite the main entrance, four blocks back from the base of the fountain, build your staircase from quartz stair edged with stone brick. Make it five blocks wide and seven blocks high.

STEP 6

Add two rows of pillar quartz to the top of the outside wall, one inside the other, and finish the ceiling with a single layer of stone. Add a layer of glass pane along the top of the interior walls with sea lantern above each doorway and corner. Finally, put a different colour concrete block at the top of each shop doorway.

STEP 7

Copy the layout for the internal walls from Step 1. This time use stone brick for the paths. Make sure there's a 6x3 hole around the staircase. Put a safety barrier made from glass pane around the staircase hole, leaving two blocks clear at the back to give people access to the stairs. Follow Step 2 again to make your second fountain.

STEP 8

Follow Steps 3, 4 and 6 again to recreate the entire ground floor layout on the new floor.

STEP 9

Then, outside, add a row of polished diorite seven blocks up, and a row of pillar quartz followed by a row of polished diorite around the top of the outside walls, and complete the roof using stone.

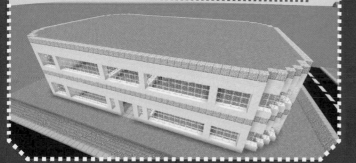

STEP 10

Lastly, add light! Five blocks in from the edges of the roof, replace four 5x15 sections of stone with glass pane. Use polished diorite to create the arches for the atrium windows. Then use glass blocks to glaze the atrium windows and make arched windows all along the length and width of the roof.

CAR PARK

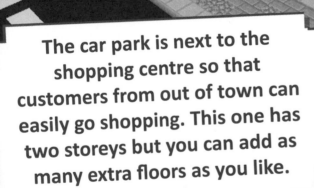

The car park is next to the shopping centre so that customers from out of town can easily go shopping. This one has two storeys but you can add as many extra floors as you like.

« SLOPES AND STAIRS »

In a real car park, the ramp between the two levels would be a gentle slope so that cars can drive easily from one floor to the next. In Minecraft, stairs always make a 45-degree angle and it's impossible to lay a flat surface over the slope. A slope this steep would be dangerous in a car park. Next time you visit a car park, look to see how gentle the slope is.

STEP 1

Four blocks back from the road, lay a 63x39 perimeter using stone slabs with a 3x3 square of stone brick in each corner. Replace the grass blocks inside the perimeter with black concrete and mark out parking spaces using white concrete. Each parking space is three blocks wide and five blocks long. Create a dotted line for where the ramp will go up to the next floor.

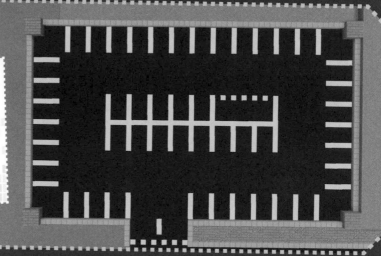

STEP 2

Next to the dotted line, build the ramp from seven rows of black and white concrete blocks placed corner to corner (diagonally). Make these rows nine blocks long, the same length as the dotted line. Add stone brick at the side to create a safety barrier — we don't want any cars to drive off the edge.

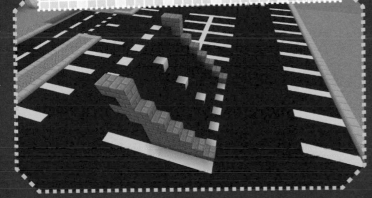

STEP 3

On the same level as the top of your ramp, lay a floor of black and white concrete, with the same markings as shown. Leave a 10x7 gap around the ramp. Edge this gap with stone brick on three sides to form another safety barrier. On top of this floor, build a perimeter wall made from stone slabs with 3x3 stone brick squares in the corners.

STEP 4

Build up the stone brick in the corners to join the ground floor with the top of the car park. Underneath the perimeter wall made from stone slabs at the top of the car park, add a row of stone brick blocks all the way around.

STEP 5

Add a safety barrier around the top floor by adding another layer of stone brick on top of your 3x3 corner squares and joining them up with a single row of stone brick all around the perimeter.

PARK

Whether they want to walk their dog, play with friends, go for a run or just sit in the sun, the people of your city will love going to the park. It's right next to the shopping centre so that people can get some fresh air and chill after shopping.

MATERIALS

« FREE PLAY »

Unlike the other builds, you don't need to stick strictly to the instructions to make sure all the parts go together. You can put different elements of the park in different places and it will still work out. Maybe you want a bigger playground, or to change the ice rink to a boating lake? The choice is yours!

STEP 1

The L-shaped playground sits in the far corner of the park opposite the shopping centre. Prepare the ground by replacing 27x15 grass blocks with sand, leaving one 6x9 corner untouched. Surround your L-shape using oak fence with oak fence gate along one short side.

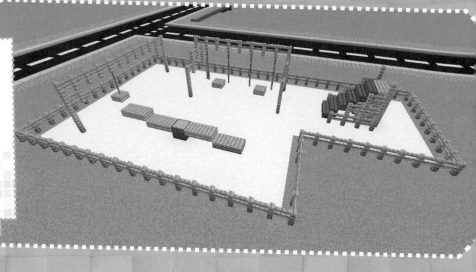

FOR REAL!

Sand provides a soft landing surface that doesn't get muddy and fencing keeps animals out and stops small children from escaping.

STEP 2

Build your slide from spruce stair and oak wood plank. Make it three blocks high and two blocks wide with fence on either side and ladders at the back.

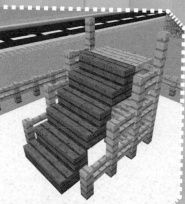

STEP 3

For the swings, build a frame from oak fence and each swing from iron bars and oak wood slab.

STEP 4

Make the frame for the zip wire using oak fence. Use iron bars and oak wood slab to make the seat.

sticky piston

TOP TIP!

These Minecraft versions of playground favourites are just for display but you can experiment with pistons, sticky pistons and redstone to create an all-new playground ride.

piston

redstone wire

GO WITH THE FLOW

Friction and temperature can have a dramatic effect on how objects behave; from how fast or slowly something moves to whether it exists as a liquid, solid or gas.

« N-ICE SUMMER? »

Ice rinks pop up everywhere in the winter. Like a freezer, they use electricity to keep the ice frozen. In the summer, with all that sunshine and warmth, an ice rink would use up a huge amount of electricity. Luckily, the Minecraft sun won't melt your ice rink so you can have it all year.

« FRICTION »

When you walk on a rough surface, such as grass, it locks together with the surface of your shoes, creating friction (a force that resists movement). An ice rink and ice skates both have smooth surfaces. When one smooth surface meets another, there is very little friction so you slip and slide quickly and easily.

But even though the surface of an ice rink is smooth, there is enough friction to melt it slightly. This makes it even more slippery because the thin layer of water evens out the small ridges and dips from people's skates. Which you want on an ice rink, but not when you're walking!

Skis travel fast on snow because both surfaces are very smooth.

« ICE, WATER, STEAM »

Ice is water that has frozen (or become solid) because it's gone below its freezing point of 0 °C (32 °F). As ice warms up, it melts. This means there's always a thin layer of water on the surface of an ice rink because there's always warmer air above it.

If water is heated to its boiling point of 100 °C (212 °F), it starts to bubble and escape as steam. Think of a boiling kettle or pan. When steam hits a cold surface, such as a window, it condenses, forming drops of liquid again.

This picture shows H_2O as ice (a solid), water (a liquid) and steam (a gas).

STEP 6

Next, create the ice rink. It's in the corner nearest the car park. Starting six blocks from each edge of the park, dig out a rectangle 20x30 and round off the corners. Then fill the hole with ice.

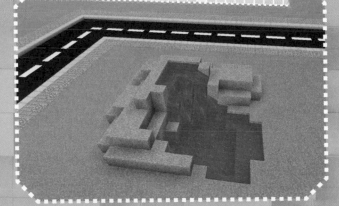

STEP 5

Use oak wood for the centre of the seesaw and oak wood plank for the sides.

STEP 7

Edge the ice with a safety barrier made from hay bales, leaving spaces for the entrance and exit. Put oak fence across the entrance and exit and make lighting from oak fence and glowstone.

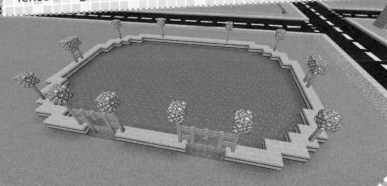

STEP 8

In the corner opposite the car park and next to the ice rink, make a decorative water feature. Use stone block to create an irregular pile of rocks, with different levels for the water to cascade down from. Dig a hole for your pool in front of the rocks. Touch the top with a water bucket to start the water flowing.

STEP 9

Right click with your shovel to create a path. Replace grass with dirt block and sprinkle seeds and bonemeal to grow flowers and crops.

PERFECT PATTERNS

Designers and architects think very carefully about the shapes they use to decorate and cover surfaces. From paving slabs to roof tiles, there are tessellating shapes everywhere.

≪ TILES AND TESSELLATIONS ≫

The piazza is tiled with shapes that fit together perfectly. Any shape that can be repeated to fill an area without leaving any gaps is said to 'tessellate'. All wall and floor tiles are made of tessellating shapes, such as squares, rectangles and hexagons.

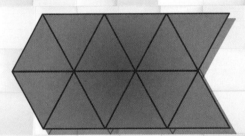

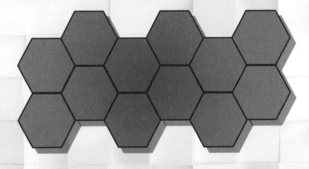

Equilateral triangles, hexagons and squares tessellate.

These are not the only shapes that tessellate, though. There are some you might not immediately think of:

Some irregular shapes tessellate.

A pattern can even be made from two or more shapes that tessellate together:

Pairs of different shapes can tessellate too.

STEP 10

In the corner of the park closest to the shopping centre, you're going to build a piazza with decorative paving and a fountain. Around 15 blocks in from the edges of the park, build the base for the fountain. Dig out a circle with a radius of six blocks (that's the distance from the edge to the centre) and line it with stone brick. Add a stone brick wall around the outside edge to keep the water in.

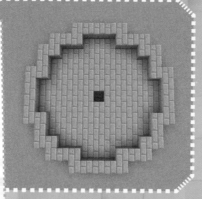

STEP 11

Now add paving around the fountain in a symmetrical design, using different colours. We have placed polished andesite and polished granite in horizontal, diagonal and vertical rows that are eight blocks long, but you could use different blocks and create your own design.

STEP 12

To follow this design, lay polished diorite around the edges of your rows, making it two blocks wide around the straight edges and one block wide around the diagonals.

STEP 13

Fill in the gaps with P-shaped designs made from stone brick and polished granite and finish off the edges with more polished diorite.

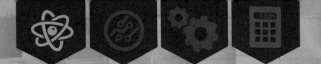

THE STUFF OF LIFE

Everything needs help to grow, develop and thrive – in both Minecraft and the real world. Plants provide food for lots of animals (and people) so let's find out more about them...

≪ HOW PLANTS WORK ≫

Most plants have roots, a stem and leaves. Many also have flowers some of the time.

The roots keep the plant firmly in place in the ground. Water and nutrients from the soil enter the plant through the roots. They travel along the stem to reach the growing tips of the plant and the leaves.

The leaves contain a substance called chlorophyll which uses the energy from sunlight, water carried up from the roots and gases from air to make food for the plant. Chlorophyll is green, which is why most plants are green.

To reproduce, many plants make seeds. Others split apart or grow new plants from roots that spread underground. Plants that make seeds have flowers.

flower — stem

leaves — root

≪ WHAT PLANTS NEED ≫

In Minecraft, we can make plants and flowers grow by sprinkling bonemeal on the grass. In the real world, plants and flowers grow from seed, so to add flowers to your grass you would need to sow some seed. Plants also need sunlight, water and soil in order to grow.

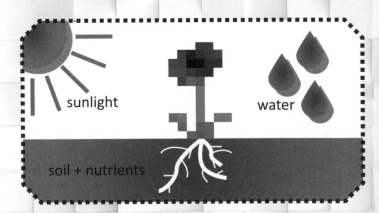

sunlight — water — soil + nutrients

≪ BRILLIANT BONE ≫

Farmers and gardeners often use fertiliser to help plants grow better. Fertiliser is a special plant food that has nutrients (useful chemicals) in it. Bone meal, which is made from ground-up animal bones, is a great fertiliser. The nutrients in it are more concentrated (stronger) than the nutrients in the soil so they help plants to grow strong and healthy.

bone meal

STEP 14

Add a pyramid of stone blocks three blocks high and five blocks wide to the middle of the fountain. Then right click the top with a water bucket and water will start to flow down into the base.

STEP 15

Add paths to help people find their way around the park. To turn grass into a grass path, right-click on the grass block with a shovel. The paths should be winding rather than straight and they should link all parts of the park.

STEP 16

Finally, plant trees around the park, wherever you think they will look good. To grow longer grass and flowers, sprinkle bonemeal around the park.

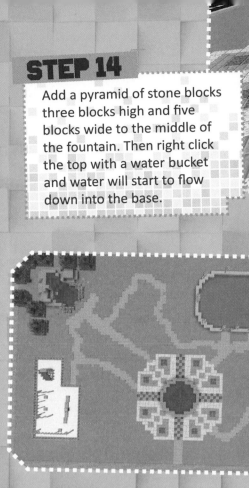

GLOSSARY

ABSORB
To take in.

AIR CONDITIONING
A system that keeps a building cool.

ANTENNAE
An aerial for receiving radio signals.

ARCHITECT
A person who designs buildings.

ATRIUM
A space inside a building that's open-air or covered with a skylight.

CIRCUIT
A path that an electrical current can flow through.

CIRCUMFERENCE
The length of the edge of a circle.

CONDUCT (ELECTRICITY, HEAT)
To carry.

DIAMETER
A line across a circle, through the centre, dividing it in half.

DIMENSIONS
Measurements (e.g. on a plan).

DISTORT
To stretch something out of shape.

EARTHQUAKE
A movement of the ground caused by events deep in the Earth.

ELECTROMAGNETIC WAVES
Waves that travel through space (or matter) including radio waves, visible light waves and microwaves.

EQUILATERAL TRIANGLE
A triangle with sides of equal length and the same size angles.

EXCAVATE
To dig up and out of the ground.

FOOTPRINT
The area on the ground occupied or overhung by a building.

FOUNDATIONS
Underground support for a building or other structure.

FRICTION
A force that prevents or slows down the movement of one surface over another.

HYDRAULIC
Powered by a system of compressed fluids (liquid or gas).

INSULATION
Material that doesn't carry heat, used to keep something warm (because the heat is trapped).

ISOSCELES TRIANGLES
A triangle with two equal sides, and two angles the same size.

MICROWAVES
A form of electromagnetic radiation, often used for heating up food.

OCTAGON
A shape with eight straight sides.

PARALLELOGRAM
A four-sided shape with opposite sides that are parallel and the same length as each other.

PERIMETER
The total distance around the edge(s) of a shape.

PROPORTION
The correct relationship between two measurements.

RADIUS
A line from the centre of a circle to the edge (circumference).

RUBBLE
Small rocks and pieces of stone .

SCALE
The relationship between the size of something to its size in a plan. A scale of 1:100 means one unit (1 cm) on a plan stands for 100 units (1 m) of the building.

SENSOR
A device that detects movement sound, light or temperature.

SKYSCRAPER
A very tall building.

SOUNDPROOFING
Material used to stop sound.

STIMULUS
Something (such as sound, light or heat) that causes a reaction.

STOREY
A floor (level) in a building.

STRUTS
Supports that strengthen a building or structure.

TESSELLATE
To fit together in a regular pattern with no gaps left in between.

VIEWING PLATFORM
A place to stand to see a long way, or overlook a particular place.

X-RAY
A form of electromagnetic radiation, often used for looking inside the body.